# RUNNING
# ON EMPTY

*Books by Robert Phillips*

# RUNNING ON EMPTY

## *New Poems*

## Robert Phillips

DOUBLEDAY & COMPANY, INC.
GARDEN CITY, NEW YORK
1981

Excerpt from "The Love Song of J. Alfred Prufrock" in *The Complete Poems and Plays* 1909–1962 by T. S. Eliot is reprinted by permission of Harcourt Brace Jovanovich, Inc.

Library of Congress Cataloging in Publication Data
Phillips, Robert S.
    Running on empty.
    I. Title.
PS3566.H5R8       811'.54
ISBN: 0-385-17304-0 (trade)
ISBN: 0-385-17305-9 (paper)
Library of Congress Catalog Card Number 80-2429

For JOYCE AND RAY

# ACKNOWLEDGMENTS

The author wishes to thank the Corporation of Yaddo for a grant of time and space which helped enable this book to take shape.

Thanks is also due to the following publications, where many of the poems appeared, often in different form:

*American Poetry Review*: "My Unicorn"
*Attention Please*: "Odd Fellows Cemetery"
*Carleton Miscellany*: "The Performance" and "John Wilde's 'Happy, Crazy American Animals . . .'"
*Croton Review*: "Becoming a Giraffe"
*The Hudson Review*: "Vertical & Horizontal," "Once," "Running on Empty," and "The Whip" (under the title "Snap. Crackle. Pop")
*Images*: "Everyone Recalls the Saints, But What of the Animals?"
*Inquiry*: "A Map of Misreading," "Flatworms," and "The Silent Man"
*Massachusetts Review*: "Sunday Dinner" (under the title "Sunday Ritual")
*Modern Poetry Studies*: "Switchman at the North Station"
*The New Yorker*: "The Mole" and "Middle Age: A Nocturne"
*Ontario Review*: "Lump," "Woodchuck Redux," and "Figures of the Past"
*The Paris Review*: "The Land: A Love Letter"
*The Partisan Review*: "Amy Jones' 'A Bouquet for Judy'"
*Poetry Now*: "The Pruned Tree" and "The Fenceless Gate"
*Shenandoah*: "A Letter to Auden" and "Milton Avery's 'Sea Grasses and Blue Sea'"

*Tar River Poetry*: "A Handful of Beans"

*Xanadu:* "Once Upon a Time" and "The Unfalling"

"Lump" was reprinted in *Anthology of Magazine & Yearbook of American Poetry*, 1980; "Amy Jones' 'A Bouquet for Judy'" and "A Letter to Auden" were reprinted in the 1981 edition of the same anthology.

Special thanks to my editor, Barbara Trainer, and my friend Jerome Mazzaro, for valuable suggestions. Thanks, too, to Jackson Browne, for the title.

# CONTENTS

*If you want to write the truth,
you must write about yourself.
I am the only real truth I know.*
                              —Jean Rhys


*Remember what it was to be me:
that is always the point.*
                              —Joan Didion

# I

# MIDDLE AGE NOCTURNES

# A LEAF

I sit on cool cement,
a bench in Benrath Park,
West Germany,

and watch a *Märchen
Mädchen* approach
her mother, to proffer

a single leaf. Mother,
furiously knitting
some great woolly thing,

will not acknowledge.
The girl twirls, dances
away undaunted:

"*Aber es* ist *ein Blättchen!*"
("But it *is* a little leaf!")
she coos. And such is

the insouciance I'd like
to have, and the poem
I'd like to give to you.

# THE LAND: A LOVE LETTER

This hill and the old house on it
are all we have. Two acres,
more or less—half crabby lawn,
half field we mow but twice a year.

Some trees we planted, most gifts
of the land. The pine by the kitchen?
Grown twice as fast as our son. The bald
elm lost the race with my own hairline.

The mulberry—so lively with squirrels,
chipmunk chases, and birds—
fell like a tower in the hurricane.
My chain saw ate fruitwood for weeks.

And the juniper, the one that all but
obliterated the view? Men cut it
down to make way for the new well and water
pump. That pump should pump pure

gold: we lay awake engineering
ways to get it paid for. But we'll never
leave this mortgaged hill: This land
is changing as we change, its face

erodes like ours—weather marks,
stretch marks, traumas of all sorts.
Last night a limb broke in the storm.
We still see it limn the sky.

We've become where we have been.
This land is all we have, but this love
-letter is no more ours than anyone's
who ever married the land.

# AUTUMN CROCUS

Basketing leaves during earth's
annual leaf-taking, we realize
with a start—something's missing.
The autumn crocus that would spring

each October by these rocks,
no longer here! We never planted
them, but they implanted themselves
on us. Now, for their lack,

we are poorer. Purest orchid color,
they astonished amidst the season's
dwindling. Crocus in autumn?
How perverse! To reverse the seasons!

Every year we bore a bunch
into the house with pride,
surprising guests who'd never seen
their likes. They thought them

foreign, remote, inaccessible—
like edelweiss. No vase, glass, or jar
ever contained them. Their soft white stems
always bent, jack-eared blossoms

lolled like heads of old folks
sleeping in rocking chairs.
I read once where their yellow pistils
are a saffron source. For us,

source of satisfaction. Now gone.
A woodchuck? Early frost?
My failure to care for bulbs?
They were the unaccountable

we thought we could count on.

# THE UNFALLING

*(after Ted Kooser)*

November fifteenth, and still no fall
of leaves. They cling tenaciously
to every branch and stem. Weeks ago
they turned color, now turncoat
and will not let go. Even last night's
*Sturm and Drang* left them, unperturbed.

In the country the bushel baskets
are impatient, awaiting their legacies,
their windfalls. Wheelbarrows stand
unmoving. Each suburban garage and cellar
houses rakes and yard brooms which lean
upon one another, mourning next-of-kin.

The gutters at my roofline are amazed:
Each autumn they strangle on leaves—
yet last night's rain set them singing
clear and high, a castrati choir.
All the baseballs boys lost last summer
long to be blanketed down for winter . . .

   Will the leaves never fall?
Will this be the fall that failed?

# THE SILENT MAN

*Speech is dirty silence.*
—WALLACE STEVENS

Silence is not golden.
Is whitest white—
an untrampled snowfield.

Not silence of the grave:
peace before a storm.
Hush before utterance.

Silence of possibility.
Taciturn, I preserve
stillness. Soundlessness.

Try, I invite you. Seal
your lips. Hold your breath.
Keep unruffled the white

velvet cloak of silence.
Some people will say,
He was struck dumb! No,

there simply is nothing
to say worth breaking
this white silken web.

# THE PERFORMANCE

Spring tumbles down
like circus clowns
from a trick automobile.
Red, yellow, blue blurs
spill over the ground.
The air fills with zany
beauty. No Barnum and Bailey
more spectacular, spring
juggles, springs hand
-springs, rides a dapple
bareback beneath a tent
of blue, walks a silver
high wire without any net,
waves, teeters, trips,
and plunges through
the summer air straight
toward a hard cold fall.

# ONCE UPON A TIME

In Europe they lived like princess and prince,
not in a palace, though one graced the block,
and on Sundays they strolled in its gardens.
They gazed Narcissus-like into its pools;
their daughters chased mallards and rare black swans.

Their own house was a redone half-mansion
they couldn't hope to occupy in the States;
a winding staircase spun three stories high;
the windowpanes told bright, stained-glass fables;
the latticed gazebo in the back yard

bore roses which she watered every day
(*"Jeden Tag!"* their avuncular landlord
ordered, and she groaned but watered daily).
Participants in some vague fairy tale,
they walked the Rhine with the dressed-up Germans

and made wild love on their goose-feather bed.
Griffins and unicorns figured their dreams.
In two years they saw but two meager snows,
as those roses grew and their daughters grew,
and when they returned to America

she lost him, he lost her— Where did they go?

# FIGURES OF THE PAST

*(to the memory of Nell Claire Kunker)*

"In your memory it is
   always summertime,
   sunlight bright but pastel.
   We have soft edges.
   Were you to touch us
   (it is *you* we find touching),
   we would be velvet, dust
   -pussies, woodland moss.
   Even fine-focus cannot correct.

"We have no substance.
   We exist only in mind.
   Our diet, an inheritance
   of air. To imagination's movement
   we dance the synapse shuffle:
   First teacher, first date,
   Great-grandfather, lost love—
   forever old, forever young—
   we are here. Waiting. Accounted for.

"Unwind, rewind, rerun us at will.
   We are a past of your reconstruction,
   figments, Ophelias to your Hamlet.
   History is rewritten daily.
   Even as you read this
   we are perceptibly fading.
   You will become one of us."

# MIDDLE AGE: A NOCTURNE

The silver tea service
assembles, stands at attention
when you walk by.
Like some lost regiment,
it wears tarnished coats.

The grand piano bares
yellowed teeth as you
give it the brush-off.
You no longer tickle its fancy.
The feeling is mutual.

The liquor cabinet chokes
on dusty bottles. You're forbidden.
In the wines sediment
settles like sentiment,
like expectations.

You visit your children's rooms.
In their sleep they breathe
heavily. In their waking
they bear new adulthood
easily. They don't need you.

In her dreams your wife sheds
responsibilities like cellulite,
acquires a new habit.
A gaunt nun of the old order,
she bends to a mystical flame.

All the pictures have been
looked at, all the books read.
Your former black mistress,
the telephone, hangs around;
there's no one you want to call.

But early this morning,
in the upper field:
seven young deer
grazing in the rain!

# II

# NINETY MILES
# FROM NOWHERE

# NINETY MILES FROM NOWHERE

(*for Elinor Cubbage*)

*And even if you were in some prison
the walls of which let none of the
sounds of the world come to your senses—
would you not then still have your
childhood?*
—RAINER MARIA RILKE

*We are all of us what we are to be
by the time we are ten years old.*
—SØREN KIERKEGAARD

## 1    *Vertical & Horizontal*

Mother grew up in the Blue Ridge,
thriving on the various landscape,
Southern sounds, the thin air.
He married her, brought her heirlooms,
antiques, pretensions back to Delaware,
back to the only town he ever knew
or felt comfortable in. Mother fell
in love with a uniform, not knowing
how uniform life could be.

Ensconced, immediately she felt oppressed
as teacher's wife, and by the heavy air.
 (Could a soufflé ever rise in it?)
"It's not so much the heat," she remarked,
"it's the humility." The landscape?
 Unrelentingly flat—not one hill
within ninety miles. The natives'
accent? Flat. The townspeople? Flat
-footed. Even the songbirds songed off-key.

Father never noticed—he,
whose favorite catch was flounder.
Every morning for decades she rose,
deflated, a vertical soul snared
within an horizontal landscape,
knowing a steamroller had run over her life.
And once a year Mother returned
to Virginia, head lifted high, and pretended
she never had come down in this world.

## 2   *The Pruned Tree*

Father announced, "I must prune
that tree . . ." and in my six-year-old
head he ceremoniously hung,
like Christmas tree ornaments,
a prune from every branch.

How wonderful for the birds,
I thought. And how could weather
hurt the fruit, it being already
so badly wrinkled? I delighted
in the dream of my pruned tree.

He went out, cut to the quick
every lively limb. My tree stood naked,
ashamed, unfruitful. And next season,
when it grew sticky shoots everywhere,
I did not look or care.

## 3  *Sunday Dinner*

That silver gravy
boat was all afloat
with giblets till Father
helped himself. His ladle
fished full fathom five.
Four children bated
breaths, waited, faces
clean and wide as China
plates. We memorized
Father dipping all—
all the gizzard,
all the liver parts—
then saw the lonely heart
get drowned in his potato
dam before he passed
the burgled gravy on.

# 4  *The Mole*

"There goes the Mole!" Mother cried.
"You children look quick or you'll miss
   him!" It was Father, disappearing down
   the cellar stairs. Every day he'd retreat
   to his radio shack, stay past midnight.

He'd built a rig others envied, came
   from miles around to see. Every day
   he'd jam the airwaves, ruin the block's TV.
   Every day we'd hear him sit before the mike
   calling "CQ, CQ, calling CQ" to whoever
   listened at the other end. He once
   claimed to reach Moscow. "Ralph's the handle,
   calling from W2CAT, the Old Cat Station—
   W-2-CAT-Alley-Tail." He *was* a handsome cat;
   Mother once adored him, I know.

But what I'll never know is, Why he'd talk
   to any stranger far away and not once
   climb back up the stairs to the five of us
   to say, "Hello . . . hello . . . hello . . . hello . . . hello."

## 5    *The Fenceless Gate*

In Laurel, Delaware—the town
I grew up in—there stood a house
surrounded by a yard that had a gate
without a fence. No one could tell
if the gate once had had a fence that fell,

stranding the gate. No one could tell me
if there ever existed a fence. Every day
I passed that gate without a fence,
and wondered. I was a boy too shy
to ask the ladies who lived there.

To ask, I would have had to stop
before the gate, unlatch the latch,
open the gate, walk through, close the gate,
latch the latch. When all the time,
I could walk around. Foolish, either way.

No one else in Laurel, Delaware, seemed to think
it odd. Were there other houses in other towns
with gates without fences? Was it a "style"?
I lost sleep: I dreamed sashes without windows,
windows without houses, roofs without coops,

stanchions without barns. I plotted
to pull that gate down! Then one day the gate
without a fence appeared in Ripley's
*Believe It or Not!* And I rejoiced.
In taking notice, at least Ripley was with me.

## 6   *Once*

"Mother, what is Labor Day?" I once
asked. "That, my dear, is when everybody

else in the country goes to the beach
except us," she said over her heavy iron,

her heavy irony. Why everybody else,
not us? Was there a national lottery?

Had our family, like blind Pew, drawn
the black spot? If not this year, could we

go the next? It was years before I understood.
One year we went to the beach. A new world,

half an hour away. I never had seen
the ocean. My big toe in the Atlantic!

Mother and the four of us on the beach,
Father on the boardwalk on a bench,

under an umbrella, wearing a ratty straw hat.
Suddenly he was somebody's old aunt!

(Once he'd gotten sun poisoning fishing,
he claimed.) He looked at his wristwatch a lot.

Mother wore an ancient wool bathing suit,
her legs thin as the stork's.

I leapt repeatedly into the muscled sea,
the sea rumpled, my brothers romped,

the sun felt good, the salt smelt good,
Jesus! it was fun, and we never went back.

## 7   *The Whip*

I will hire a master builder
to reconstruct my childhood
home. There will, first of all,
be a well-painted white bathroom

door directly opposite a tan
cellar door. That is essential.
On the inside of the bathroom door
the builder must screw a fat brass

hook and hang there a thick
braided horsewhip. Every time
I opened the bathroom door,
it swayed gently, like doom:

Leather. Heavy. A stinger
at the tip. That whip was the end
of all fear and fear of punishment
whenever Father flew up the cellar

stairs, raging—whenever childhood
brawls disturbed his solitude.
Father yanked down our pants, flailed
the air. Mother went and hid somewhere.

Once he broke it on my brother,
went to Public Landing, bought another.
Today I had drinks with Father.
We exchanged old jokes, pleasantries;

yet underfoot I heard feet pounding
up the stairs. Overhead,
that flicked lightning in the air.

## 8 A *Handful of Beans*

*What shall I learn of beans
or beans of me?*
—HENRY DAVID THOREAU

I was a boy when first I heard
Boston called "Beantown."
I didn't think "baked beans"—
imagined instead a town
where streets were strung
with string beans. The opposite
of golden heaven—the vines
would trip me on my way
to school, my assignments lost
forever in green gutters.

Next I read "You are what you eat."
And thought, I am a bean, a human bean.
At night I dreamed myself walking
around town, a green Mister Peanut,
Mister Peanut with gangrene.
An unjolly Green Giant.

For years I had to pick them
on Grandfather's dirt farm.
Pole beans dangled genitalia,
bunch beans brought me to my knees.
Temperatures over one hundred,
no shade, noontime we broke

for lunch—cornbread and beans,
or that vegetable mismarriage,
succotash. I couldn't eat.

Then back to beans. I dreamed
Jack Beanstalk's beans, how
they transported him above
his poor world to the goose
that laid golden eggs.
Grandfather's beans did no
uplifting magic, drove me
deeper down. I wanted to swim—
a lily on the millpond! To read—
a fashionable white figure
in a shaded white hammock. Instead,
beans. They had a long season.

If I picked enough, Grandpa
would respect me. If I ate enough,
Grandma would love me. In high school
I saw *East of Eden* twice,
near-died when James Dean's beans
failed to buy his father's heart.
Another bean betrayal.

Even today I cannot eat them
without the mush of summer
in my mouth: farm poverty,
hog swill, chicken shit.
Come, I can show you unhappiness
in a handful of beans.

# 9 *Magic*

My magic apparatus, my bag of tricks,
rests in the basement now. Cotton-batting rabbit,
mystical linking rings, multiplying billiard balls,
vanishing silk handkerchiefs, feather bouquets—
the preoccupations of a childhood spirited away—
beckon, Svengali-fashion, still.
The lure of chicanery remains.

Stored there, those pretty deceptions,
those fabulous feats of legerdemain,
should seem tawdry to me now.
All lacquer, gilt, and glitter cannot conceal
the illusion of illusions. Only children deceive
and are themselves not deceived.
The adult mind discovers the trick.

Any day was a good day to practice my magic.
A corner of the attic was reserved
for the black table, its embroidered silver moons
ordered from some Philadelphia prestidigitator.
I was a moon gazer night and day!
Hours then disappeared for a boy
behind a necromantic table:

It didn't matter if the boy could not hit
a home run, perfect a flying tackle.
Every day had a false bottom.

The mawking outside could not reach
that enchanted tower with its conjurer.
But, magician, charmer, pale wizard,
you practiced your tricks too well:

Sleight of hand must be outgrown.
Mere magic cannot stay the mind.
The boy becomes a man of shopworn tricks,
in a world with no trapdoor.

## 10    *The Suit of Clothes*

"Ida, the boy should have
a suit of clothes,"
Uncle Harlow sighed,
hearing I had no suitable
clothes for Sunday School.

My wardrobe? Khaki wash
-pants, Fruit of the Loom
underwear, and hand-me-down
Army shirts from Mother's
brother to mine, then to me.

Upon the four-poster bed
lay all his "suits of clothes"—
bankers' suits, gangster chalk stripes,
padded shoulders, pointed lapels—
and afterward, for all his kindness,

I skulked to Sunday School
encased in blare-blue serge that itched;
pants big enough for three pairs of jeans;
pads, lapels, and outsized double-breasts
that anyone could tell would never suit.

The very name was odd. Did you have
to be an "odd" fellow to lie there?
I went with a gang of boys,
out of curiosity. The richest grave
-yard in town, the most manicured,
"noted" for its elaborate gravestones,
a mausoleum or two (so named,
I know now, for old King Mausolus—
whose widow erected over his sarcophagus
one of the Seven Wonders of the World).
"*This* man must have been very great,"
I said before an imposing stone.
"*This* one was even greater. He got statues!"
Before I knew money could buy anything,
I thought a lofty stone proclaimed
a president, a genius, a king.

And I went there with family who placed
plastic flowers on a marker not nearly
so big as I would have liked.
(Why couldn't our family have a mausoleum,
too? A stone house in which to lie, stately,
on a stone shelf, instead of underground?)
"There's where Grandfather will lie,
and next to him Grandmother, and little Mary.
And over yonder, places for your father,
and for me." (Mother always said she wanted
to be buried in Virginia, underneath a spreading

cherry tree, in her family plot. But she
was resigned to this shadeless, sand-flead lot.)

"And what about me?" I begged. A cloud crossed
the sky. Eyes scanned the tidy cemetery,
surrounded by chain link. So many deep
shadows cast by so many stones! So many
miniature American flags, flapping, faded!
It seemed to house an exclusive fraternity.
"Oh, there's no room for you," they said.
"No room left. You'll have to make provisions
of your own." And the wind crackled
the grasses, and the words chilled my heart.
I never felt so excluded in my life.

## 12   *Running on Empty*

As a teenager I would drive Father's
Chevrolet cross-county, given me

reluctantly: "Always keep the tank
half full, boy, half full, ya hear?"

The fuel gauge dipping, dipping
toward Empty, hitting Empty, then

—thrilling!—'way below Empty,
myself driving cross-county

mile after mile, faster and faster,
all night long, this crazy kid driving

the earth's rolling surface,
against all laws, defying chemistry,

rules, and time, riding on nothing
but fumes, pushing luck harder

than anyone pushed before, the wind
screaming past like the Furies . . .

I stranded myself only once, a white
night with no gas station open, ninety miles

from nowhere. Panicked for a while,
at standstill, myself stalled.

At dawn the car and I both refilled. But,
Father, I am running on empty still.

# III

---

# A MODERN
# GALLERY

# A LETTER TO AUDEN

About suffering you were wrong, Wystan,
you who understood so much of this world,
went askew on its human position;
how suffering occurs, how people react.
It is true that in Brueghel's "Icarus,"
for instance, everything *does* turn away
quite leisurely from the disaster. But:

Who has not seen countless real instances
where crowds, riveted to an accident,
try to save the bodies from the wreckage;
dive icy green waters for the drowning;
weep genuine tears at a stranger's fire?
All had somewhere to get to, but instead,
knowing that there but for the grace of God . . . ,
tarried to share the human condition.

# A MAP OF MISREADING

The old poet's face
was a street map
opened and closed
so many times,
so many ways,
no one could read
what was going on
between the lines.

His official biographer
handed us a new map,
smoothed of all irregularities.
No non-conforming blocks.
No dead ends. And no underground.

# ALLEN GINSBERG APPEARS BEARDLESS

*Cover*, American Poetry Review,
VIII, 3 (1979)

The shock! It's Wallace Stevens
without pinstripes, Emily Dickinson
without white. It's T. S. Eliot
without a collar, Marianne Moore
without a hat. It's Wystan Auden
without wrinkles, Doc Williams
without stethoscope. It's
Emperor Bly without a serape,
Robinson Jeffers in a bowling shirt,
Dame Edith Sitwell in a miniskirt!
How can our poetry survive
such a close shave?

# THE DEATH OF JANIS JOPLIN

*(October 4, 1970)*

Because she was a white girl
        born black and blue,
because she was outsized victim
        of her own insides,
because she was voted
        "Ugliest Man on Campus,"
because she looked for something
        and found nothing—
        She became famous.

"Tell me that you love me!"
        she screamed at audiences.
They told. Fat Janis wouldn't
        believe. Twenty-seven,
a star since twenty-four,
        she tried to suck, lick,
smoke, shoot, drip, drop,
        drink the world.
        Nothing worked.

Bought a house, a place
        to go home to.
Bought a dog, something to give
        love to. Nothing worked.

Jimi Hendrix died, Janis cried—
    "Goddamn. He beat me
to it." Not by much. Three weeks
    later she joined him.
        Part of something at last.

# A MODERN GALLERY

1   *John Wilde's "Happy, Crazy American Animals
    and a Man and Lady at My Place"*

A portly possum dangles by his tail
from my living-room rafter. He adroitly assails
reality from topside, where inquiring crows nest.
The fox in stony stance upon my chest
of drawers looks stuffed, but his bark of love
is such stuff as dreams are made of.

Brilliant-hued birds and somber bats
fly overhead. Underfoot a domiciled wildcat
bats a ball across my planks, beneath my eaves,
but those furry forepaws' claws are sheathed.
The panoplied armadillo has seized
upon shards of a vase which once I prized—

Oh, the vanity of earthly possessions!
The vase was broken in the animals' procession
that toppled my turvy vanity upon its side.
Which is real? The fox and armadillo, or I?
I think there's a leopard behind that door.
The back door is open still. Are there *more?*

A polar bear lurches to embrace me like a brother.
Wild ducks fly in one window and out the other,
following an inner weather I cannot know.

My house is modest. The plaster falls like snow.
It was my sanctuary, legacy for kin.
What kinship with these beasts, clamoring in?

Antediluvian arteries pulse in time and quick
with those of a naked lady, prime and pink,
now prancing in step with the great horned stag;
the beat of their marching does not lag,
parading princely across cracked linoleum.
Something in her high society succumbs.

All out-of-doors wants in, all in-of-doors, out.
Something wild in the mildest of us shouts.
These creatures, sniffing in strange civility,
would huddle close and comfort us, if they could.

## 2   Amy Jones' "A Bouquet for Judy"

Someone placed this bouquet upon the waters.
    Casual flowers meant to cheer. Childhood colors:
pink, yellow, green, blue. Lovable, touching. A starfall.

It is a bridal bouquet tossed away in ecstasy.
    It is a floral tribute never delivered to a talent.
It exists upon a plane beyond ecstasy and talent.

See how it is wrapped in (news?) paper, floating.
    See how it has nothing to do with news, floating.
See how it is neither above or below, real or unreal.

Surely it is rooted, this bouquet of cut flowers,
    In the feminine soul. But—and do not miss it—
a sailboat. Small, white, it floats just beyond:

the male force billowing and blossoming. Bouquet and boat,
    uniting opposites within the celestial light shining,
within the biggest flower's magical black eye.

Look into the eye of the flower, into the eye
    of God, the I of God. Bouquet and boat, flower and I,
real and unreal, male and female, all have become one.

### 3  Morris Graves' "Joyous Young Pine"

Silently, and all alone, with no one
    to witness before the moon's fine scrim,
the pine in jubilation lifts its limbs.

It is an exultant young priest, praying.
    In spirit it is a Zen master, praying.
The moon, its halo of immateriality.

Such strange textures, strange rhythms!
    White threads of moonlight, white writing
in the sky! Joy of the human heart.

Here wind soughs in greeny boughs.
    Here dew seeps through dry earth.
Here insects creep up limbs, while

this mere stripling of a tree dances—
    David before the Ark—invoking legends,
holy delights, mysteries.

## 4   Milton Avery's "Sea Grasses and Blue Sea"

The world is flat. Its colors uniform.
Its shapes geometric. Was nature ever more abstract?
More than abstract—inert. The opposite of Van Gogh's
"Starry Night," where even the sky roars like the sea.

Beneath that slender strip of unmoving sky,
the seascape is but two blue trapezoids—
the grasses, pale mirror of the sky,
the water, essence of all blue.

It is the waves one never forgets
(once shocked into recognizing them!)—
Avery's brave black waves in a blue blue sea.
For years I thought they were rocks:

ominous projections. Not so. Waves—
blacker than boulders, roughly rimmed,
flecked with only a suggestion of foam.
*Blackcaps* as far back as the eye can see!

Avery's black is the color of all light,
radiant as the whitest of whites.

# IV

---

# A BESTIARY

# V

---

# SURVIVAL SONGS

# WOODCHUCK REDUX

*(for my friend and son, Graham Phillips)*

A shadow of his summer self, diminished
as the winter (which retreats,
tail between its legs), my woodchuck

makes a comeback, choosing Easter
resurrection. He's come to hog
my ground. No question, he will stay.

He sits upright on the grass, keeping watch
for anything edible. Chucked
of my largesse, he undulates a few feet

and nips a hyacinth in the bud.
Winter I thought I was shed of him.
In my mind I replanted all.

Now he awaits beneath my back window,
short ears, short tail, long memory.
I stomp; he answers with a whistle.

At sunset, getting scotched, I think:
I could put out poison, something
I've never done. My luck,

I'd only get his mate. Old Chuck,
we'll fight it out one more year.
I'll plant, you'll eat, both standing our ground.

# FLATWORMS

In biology class we decapitated them,
scissoring their bodies in two.
We boys had fun; girls cringed or gagged.

Yet within a week each half gave rise
to a new half: head on one blind stump,
and head, too, on the severed midsection.

Each head with brain and eyes, good as new.
Miracle enough the worms survived.
More miracle, their recapitulation.

I named mine John the Baptist, Anne Boleyn,
Sir Thomas More, and Mary Queen of Scots,
and marveled that such wriggling things

accomplished what queens and martyrs could not.

# SHARKS

*(for Tom Baker)*

Everybody should abhor them.
Carnivores, the slightest have teeth
like slicing blades. Boneless,
they collapse when captured.
It is impossible to take their exact measure.

There are two hundred fifty species.
Living fossils, their ancestors scavenged
Crete's seas one hundred million
years ago. Yet all are vulnerable:
they must not rest a minute unsupported.

Without flotation bladder, they
are sentenced to swim to keep from sinking.
One stationary snooze, their bodies fill
with the killing water, and they drown.
Their element, their executioner.

And so it is with poets, and painters,
and an occasional sad ad-man:
In an alien landscape they survive,
by keeping on the move to stay alive.

# MY UNICORN

Today I walked through a herd of unicorns—
unicorns tossing horns across
ersatz tapestries, posters, tee shirts,
beach towels, playing cards, ashtrays.
In the stalls along Madison and Third
it is Unicorn City. They've usurped
the Schmoo and Spiro Agnew.
There is even a hat rack:
Pink-painted eunuch horns
upon which to hang your chapeaux.

These are not *my* unicorn.
A shy creature, barely glimpsed,
he races swiftly through a black forest
somewhere in Germany or France—
the whitest thing in Christendom!
No thanks to Noah he survived the Flood.
His mate died long long ago.
In his head he hears lost chorales of Monteverdi.
He dines on orchids. He is the only unicorn
in the universe, and never lonely as you or I.

# BECOMING A GIRAFFE

*(Homage: Marianne Moore)*

Last night at midnight
my skin spotted and fuzzed,
a tawny chenille lawn—
pied as a world map,
spotted as the constellation
Camelopardalis, "formal
as the scales on a fish."
Myself camouflaged,
a rope of tail, fringed
with flax, uncoiled
behind my behind. My arms
and legs quadrupeded,
delicate-hoofed knobby
poles. My head sprouted
ornaments, inverted shaving
brushes. My ears jackassed,
so my wife says, at endearing
angles. My eyes liquefied.
I became a giraffe!
Unnaturally my neck stretched
and stretched and stretched—
rubbery as Alice's—
giraffing toward heaven,
an undulating constrictor
luxuriating in an African sun.

Now I browse tall trees'
truest leaves. I nibble
short grasses' rarest blades.
Eighteen feet above it all,
I ruminate upon what has been,
what is being, what is to be.
Though I am voiceless,
do not think I have no voice:
To be a giraffe is not to be
useless. If a tired monkey
desire it, my back can carry
a monkey upon it. If a woman
in a burning building
require it, my neck can ladder
her to safety. If children are bored,
my neck can become a sliding-board.
If virgins are restless,
my beribboned neck can maypole.
If a man is stranded, my neck
can bridge troubled waters . . .
Although my attitude appears
lofty, I am "renouncing
a policy of boorish indifference."
I am warm-blooded yet. Let
this neck lift in laughter,
prinkle in pride, help whomever
life has taken by the scruff.
Today I celebrate the brother
-hood of all creatures by,
with grace, gently holding sway.

# POEM FOR PEKOE

Our lives were only half gone
when she had used up

all her nine. Time came
upon her like a sledgehammer:

her insides dropped, she
waddled like a duck,

her belly ballooned,
not with child—she'd

never kittened, early on
was "fixed." Her belly

carried cancer and stones,
her muscles too flaccid

ever to tighten again.
Her bowels moved wherever,

she who had been so
extremely fastidious.

The vet said she had
only days, not months.

But the alertness!
The grandmotherly face!

We hoped. Then she couldn't
eat. You tried everything.

She became a wire sculpture.
Still we couldn't stand

to "put to sleep"
a life that'd been family

for fourteen years—traveling
to Austria, France, Italy,

uncomplaining in her carrying
-case. I was away

the day you had to
have them do it.

When I called I said,
"What's new?"—then heard.

And though our two new cats
are handsome, I cannot

stroke them long. They
never stay in my lap

as if to say they know.

# FURS OF THE WORLD

With FURS OF THE WORLD (MINK REMODELING
OUR SPECIALTY) stenciled on its side,
the Mack truck stood for two days
on the shoulder of the road, before
a restaurant named "Eat Here or We'll Both Starve."
The driver had felt a coronary coming on.
It came. He went.

The second night a policeman came,
and a coroner. One examined the man,
the other, the truck. The cop heard
extraordinary noises from the back.
He slid the difficult doors open,
jumped: warmth, animal odors.
A sound like the keening of Irish women.

Tumbling, scurrying, out the back
of the truck came all the furs of the world:
minks (who did not wish to be remodeled),
foxes and rabbits, beavers and squirrels,
muskrats and ocelots, raccoons and lynxes,
sables and chinchillas, coyotes and possums,
even the last Bengal tiger . . .

They scrambled, alive, back to their countries.
Who would believe? The policeman told no one.
Even today they are out there, multiplying.

Even today they are in the repossessed land
we all long for. In the dark their eyes glow,
authentic emeralds in the snow. Once again
the stripped woods dazzle.

# EVERYONE RECALLS THE SAINTS,
# BUT WHAT OF THE ANIMALS?

(*for William Goyen*)

They were here before we were.
We came on the sixth day.
Their numbers are fabulous.
Their names are forgotten.

> Begin with Noah's animals—a pair
> Of every living thing that creeps
> Or crawls or runs or flies. Imagine!
> The sky dark with wings flapping,
> Wide-winged souls, the ground alive
> With creeping, crawling things!

These are totally anonymous.
Many are not. Consider:

> The dove which brought Noah a leaf, a sign.
> The birds Christ released in the temple.
> The camel which went through the needle's eye.
> The ram in the thicket sacrificed for Isaac.
> The Pascal Lamb sacrificed for all the Jews.
> The lion and the lamb which lay down together.

Then consider:

> The two fishes whose bodies fed the multitude.
> The whale which swallowed then rejected Jonah.

Jesus' donkey which carried him through Jerusalem.
The good Samaritan's ass which carried the victim.
The ox and the ass which worshipped at the manger.
Balaam's ass beaten for balking at an angel . . .

Who can deny they are much
Of the Bible's poetry?
Who can deny they are much
Of the saint's magic?
Who can deny every saint
must wrestle with his animal?

These sweet creatures, who did nothing much
But give, instruct through the ages
How man, that latecomer, should live.

# LUMP

*(for Dr. John Prutting)*

You are a hard-boiled egg. Me?
No hard-boiled detective. But,

you are what I detect one day,
what propels me to see Dr. P.

You are a death-baby, I cry.
You'll grow inside me till I die.

You are a death-toad squatting,
spitting poison into my blood.

You are a lump in the breast,
cleverly disguised as one in my arm.

You are the Big C that killed Granny,
Uncle, and now wants to kill me.

You are an inelegant swell. You,
Lump, are the creep who crept up

till they cut, leaving a stump,
my arm hacked off, a leg of lamb.

But, lump, you are "perfectly benign,"
says Dr. P., rolling you curiously

between two fingers. Lump, you
are only a torn muscle, a thing

fallen below the bicep. Lump,
you are a reminder of all fallen things:

Troy, Rome, boys who build up their bodies
only to fall, cakes in the oven.

Lump, lump, you are a hard lesson.
Learn to take one's lumps.

# TOPPED

The white pine in the meadow—
so handsome, graceful, and young—
just stopped growing at the top.
As if sawed off in its prime.
Secondary limbs tried hard
to compensate for the blow—
tangentially; unseemly.
It will never be the same.

Seeing it, I thought of him—
so handsome, graceful, and young—
struck down by stroke one morning,
like a lightning-blasted tree.
He too died first at the top.
When I go, let it be whole.

# SWITCHMAN AT THE NORTH STATION

*(for John Logan)*

All day long the big ones
come lurching in—
Erie, Lackawanna, Wabash,
Bangor Fruit, Route
of the Phoebe Snow—
names that set the blood
to sing, the heart
to hammer loud as trains
coupling in the yard.

All day long he braves
the crabwise sun, closes
eyes red to cinders
big as boulders, near 'bout,
then shuffles home
to the little woman
familiar as beans,
a six-pack of beer,
a canvas cot that throbs
and jerks at midnight,
then shuttles all the way
from North White Plains
to Santa Fe.

# THE PERSISTENCE OF MEMORY,
# THE FAILURE OF POETRY

The severed hand flutters
    on the subway track,
like a moth. No—

it is what it is,
    *a severed hand.*
It knows what it is.

And all the king's doctors
    and all the king's surgeons
put hand and stump together

again. Fingers move,
    somewhat. Blood circulates,
somewhat. "A miracle!" reporters

report. But it will only
    scratch and claw, a mouse
behind the bedroom wall. We forget.

At four a.m. the hand
    remembers: intricate musical
fingerings, the metallic

feel of the silver flute.

# THE PAINTER

Surfaces are glossed over
in my trade. I know the conspiracy
of cover-ups. I'm always in a scrape,
always in the prime of life.
The shingle, the wainscot, the trim
are the world within my world,
signposts of my estate.

Reflect on barns full of grain
in Iowa, fish houses in Maine,
covered bridges school buses cross.

Then consider my work,
how it is life-extending
to whorls and grains,
to weather-eaten paints,
time-beaten stains. Think about
solid houses of the rich,
always well painted. Remember
listing houses of the poor,
flaking or—worse—
naked as a rat's tail.
My work protects,
like a lover's arms,
embracing their very life.

Matte finish or gloss?
Oil base, latex, or water?

Sherwin-Williams covers the world.
Rust never sleeps.

My labor covers for you,
for your termite neglect,
your building with green wood,
your blindness to dry rot,
your choice of cinder block
and cheap Sheetrock.
You who wish to put on a good
face, you who wish your houses
to last a mortgage's lease,
you who have children,
think on me:

Your first house needed me,
and your last. Nothing
can stop time's process.
Even your final oak box
would last a little longer
if it wore just one of my good coats.

# "IN THIS DARK WORLD AND WIDE"

"Blind man" was a game
we played at, bluffing our way
through Kool-Aid afternoons.
I always gravitated toward you
behind the thorniest hedge,
amidst the mittened sassafras:
The blindfolds we tied then
always let in some light.

At college canes of the blind
gamely tapped like blind Pew
on the cobbles of my brain.
O miraculous feats of rectitude!
Their voyages through the icy world
were tenuous as tightrope tricks.
I never helped one cross the street.
I shuttered my venetian blinds.

Remember the morning Pop's old sow
littered three pink piglets
and a white? The albino's eyes
were milky agate marbles, blind
globs of snot. The morning after,
it was gone. The sow's belly
ballooned obscenely.
And you did not understand.

Now your accident. Seat belts
and STOP signs went forgotten.
That rear-view mirror snapped,
its sharp stem gouged, gouged
your beautiful eye. Today's the day
they strip away the gauzy blindfold.
Blindfold, blind folk, blindness un-
fold. I count to ten:

Let there be light.

# MISS CRUSTACEAN

*(for Cynthia Macdonald)*

*Each year the city of Crisfield,*
*"Seafood Capital of the Nation,"*
*sponsors an event known as the*
*National Hard Crab Derby, certainly*
*one of our nation's more bizarre*
*folk celebrations . . .*

—WILLIAM W. WARNER,
*Beautiful Swimmers*

*I should have been a pair of ragged*
*claws . . .*

—T. S. ELIOT, *The Love Song*
*of J. Alfred Prufrock*

### I

"All my life I've wanted to be
Miss Crustacean!" I said into
the microphone, into the TV
cameras just after they crowned me
beauty queen at the Crab Derby.
Afterward my brother told me
what a fool I'd made of myself—

It was the first year they'd held
a beauty pageant at the Derby:
How could I have coveted the title
"all my life"? I know, I know.

But all my eighteen years ached
for recognition some way.
All my eighteen years ached.

I always had blue limbs. In high
school I bumped into every open
locker door, my upper arms and thighs
blue with bruises, clumsiness.
In the class play I tripped
on my train, forgot my lines . . .
Not everything turned out badly:

I was a good swimmer. My best stroke,
the crawl. I struggled with one poem—
About nature being "red in tooth
and claw." I longed for
Donald Lee Scruggs to ask me
to the Junior-Senior Prom.
Donald Lee was a swimmer.

When he didn't ask me, I asked him.
Only to be told he was taking
Sue-Ellen Wheatley, captain
of the girls' basketball team.
She never bumped into anything.
Fortunately, the Crab Derby
was held on Labor Day Weekend:

I hadn't been near a locker
for three months! Not one bruise.
I possessed a certain beauty.
I was confident. And that day,

a gorgeous early September day
in Crisfield, Maryland,
I became: Miss Crustacean.

II

In the year of my reign I took
my role seriously: rode through
parades in open convertibles,
attended banquets, promoted
crab meat best I could.
The following Labor Day
I returned to Crisfield to crown
my successor (Sue-Ellen Wheatley).

When I sidled up to the throne
to place my crown upon her head,
I realized I'd walked crabwise.
That was the beginning. In the years
to follow, I caught myself scuttling
about town, nails decorated
with orange-red gloss, arms bruised
cerulean blue. Scuttle, scuttle.

(I still lived at home, an old maid.
It was my own bureau drawers bruised
me blue now.) Every day I went
to swim in the unnatural blue waters
of the YWCA. In the warm element
I waved my claws in and out.
I wanted to swim nude, my pure
white abdomen lustrous alabaster.

But the Y requires tank suits.
I tread water, I wave claws
in and out. I acquire faster open
-water speed, dive to the bottom
to bury myself. For hours
I practice my crawl. Afterward,
in direct sunlight, I blink:
my stalked eyes, nubby horns.

How I hate direct sunlight!
After swimming, famine. My life
is swimming and one constant search
for food. At the Blue Dolphin Diner
they tease about how much I eat.
Anything in a pinch. I burn
it off. My parents worry:
They say my disposition has become

. . . crabby. If only they knew!
I need a new hobby, they say.
I considered shadow boxing.
Before the mirror at night
I stand in my room, slowly jabbing
the air with my powerful right
claw. I wave it like a flag.
Jab, jab, jab.

### III
The preceding pages were written
(in my crabbed hand) some years ago.

They represent a reasonable account
of my existence for twenty years.
Today my swimming has slowed,

But my love of water never ceases.
My body, shell-white from every day
inside that sunless pool. I have lost
all interest in mating. My attitude
has hardened. I am more vague:

"She believes in the oblique,
    indirect method," I heard someone say.
True. My walk, slower, too. Yet
that supports my illusions—walking
legs slightly doubled, ready to spring!

But suddenly my life has changed.
First I feared cancer. That seemed
predetermined, the crab's pincers biting
my guts like hell. Now I know it is
something even more insidious. Everything

about me, even my brain, is . . . softening.
I lie in a darkened room in my bed
for days. I feel it at my points,
I feel it in my joints. Any moment now
my entire shell will crack and bust.

# ABOUT THE AUTHOR

Known also for his fiction, criticism, and anthologies, Robert Phillips began his writing career with poetry and for that has achieved his widest audience. His poems continue to appear in leading journals—including *The New Yorker*, *The Partisan Review*, *The Paris Review*, *The Hudson Review*, and *Poetry*. His poems also appear in numerous anthologies, most recently *The Pushcart Prize IV: Best of the Small Presses*; *New York: Poems*, edited by Howard Moss; and *80 Poets for the '80s*.

Born in Delaware in 1938, he has resided in New York State since he was eighteen. Living on the Cross River Reservoir in Katonah, in northern Westchester County, he has directed the poetry reading program at the Katonah Village Library for the past dozen years. A former editor of *Modern Poetry Studies*, he continues to serve as a contributing editor of *The Ontario Review* and an associate editor of *The Paris Review*.

Robert Phillips has been a recipient of a grant in poetry from the Creative Artists Public Service Program of New York State, as well as a Yaddo Fellowship.